metamorphosis

AF624525

Pooja Hiremath

BookLeaf Publishing

Presentation by *BookLeaf Publishing*

Web: www.bookleafpub.com

E-mail: info@bookleafpub.com

ISBN: 9789357211055

First edition 2022

DEDICATION

To Bobby - for reopening doors I'd closed on myself

PREFACE

hello me

in the shattered shards
I see a myriad collection of
who I have been
and who I can be
the image is mine to choose

sheer mini polka dotted cheeky

let me tell you
it's not fun being pink silky panties
that can't be seen.
shorts and jeans and sweats are the worst
so I live for sunny days
to peek from skirts and dresses.
tiny bow on the band, hemmed laces
I hug the curves of her cheeks
her coconut body wash lingering.
I spend my days in a dark drawer
competing with sixty-three others
to be chosen, to be given a purpose.
the others are not as pretty as me -
thongs, boybriefs and boyshorts -
but we all get one day to be shown off.
so I try to stay clean
avoiding grass stains and dirt
always ready to flash.
washed in lavender soap imported from London
being air dried on a clothing rack by the window
my dream of being admired
is marred by being pulled off hastily by him
discarded like a pair of dirty socks under the bed.

broken smile

she wears my corners up, edges straight
her eyes tell me there are no crinkles
"I'm okay"
my lips part to say
lies they let slip

plastered, stitched
I just want to beam
but I am fixed in place.
dressed in chapstick before bedtime
cherry gloss during the day
the façade doesn't uphold

when she sees him
I disappear altogether
corners and edges lining up
pressed, sealed
her eyes tell me there are no crinkles.

reflection

her unflinching dark chocolate irises stare back at me.
I want to look away, but I'm curious.

she seems familiar, like a mangled old teddy bear
in her holey hoodie and worn out jeans;
I wonder who she is.

her mascara is smudged, her lips chapped
the faded traces of laugh lines are permanently
etched;
I wonder if I can help her.

she hunches shoulders to appear diminutive
tugging at her sleeves to hide the scars on her arms;
I wonder when everything changed.

I reach out, hoping to ignite some life source
but my fingers only graze glass.

the end

he came over last night
with a wily plan to
mix his special concoction
raspberry ginger ale and Malibu
numerous servings I lost count of
but my awareness did not dim on
his hands wandering under my crop top
tugging at the waistband of my shorts
"this isn't what taking it slow means"
I thought and nimbly pulled away

"seven shots and you're still not loose!"
his dismay blared a warning in my ears
the conniving plan to imbibe
for debauchery in the bedroom
revealed his true Loki nature.

mr. lord protector

at the intersection of
six years and wishes granted
I said farewell to him
to run into your arms
when I crashed my Honda Accord.
watching my pristine white sedan
scorched in scarlet flames
was symbolic to losing my innocence -
but in your embrace I was home.
you wrapped me in your pizza blanket
handed me a glass to drown my sorrows
but in your presence I had none
inadvertently I chose you as my savior.

bonded

on the cusp of autumn transitioning to winter
my Leo and your Sagittarius sparked a heat wave.
a private picnic we held, I amusedly
watched you polish off cans of whipped cream
leaving the parfait raspberries for me.
I tempted you with nonvegan
mixed berry Pop-tarts and double stuff Oreos
and you caved.
side by side, euphorically exuding a pink and red
glow
your arm on my knee, my chin on your shoulder
the spinning world stilled -
for a perfect moment
it was just you and me.

snapshot

I memorized the way your eyes wrinkle
in glee gushing about riding El Toro,
the wide grin regaling how your mom
experiments with your shoulder-length hair -
the black halo you stow away under a Tekken cap -
your prominent laugh lines showing blurry
pictures of yourself under laser lights -
now it's all I have left.

stubborn

in the below freezing, dark February morning
on the curb between Aquaintances and More than Friends
you stood tall and unfazed like a polar bear
while I nestled deep into my black down-feather coat,
your penguin companion. with my hood on,
I was called a dementor, a reference
you couldn't defend me against.
"I watched the movies," you protested.
"how can we be friends?" I teased.
a pair, you spurred new perspectives and
I chronicled our conquests.
the carriage we shared
transported us between reality.
my diary held your place in my bed
until the last page was fed to the wind.
deprived a conclusion, I enter a
labyrinth of what might have been,
ignoring the perils of rejection.
even the wind's echoing howls
"Let go, go, oh, o…"
cannot dissuade my pursuit to
rewrite the book of us.

the unknown

I walked the narrow craggy precipice
to apologize for an invisible mistake.
"what did I do?" I whimpered.
but your apparition does not respond.
waiting for a sign of life of us
I feel the churning churlish aqua sea foam below
ready to snap me up in its tidal teeth
and all I recall is
your last salutations, "hello there"
your last farewell, "tell me when you get home safe"
the gentleman you are is evanescent
making me walk the plank now
for a sin I wish I could remedy.

say anything

it's been awhile, six weeks to be exact
our eyes lock, but the gnawing silence riles me
I brandished my vulnerability
"I don't let a lot of people in. You matter."
leashed you felt, and desired escape
leaving a chasm of ignorance in your wake.
drawbridges I constructed out of
quartz photographs of memorabilia
marble pleadings for advice
granite sorry for overstepping.
not the mechanical engineer you are
each crumbled in the widening gap between us.
as I prepared to install a grave marker
you returned to the scene.
immobile in your presence
I await an explanation for your absence
but you stare through me
I've dissolved into the sheer past
my inaudible beseeching has no effect
blink, we're strangers again.

would you?

if I called you
would you answer?
if I said I needed you
would you help pick up the pieces?

if I was a brash drunk
would you overlook my dramatic antics?
if I admitted all my imperfections
would you still accept me?

if I didn't hastily proclaim my affection
would you have stayed?
if I swallowed my words and plastered a smile
would you have been happier?

if I want to ameliorate our relationship
would you give me a second chance?

11:11

I pause at the outpouring teal fountain
in the mall to toss a quarter in
to ask to talk to you again
agnostic, but I find myself humbled
at altars praying to see you again
extra vigilant of the angel number
I want more time with you
where is my fairy godmother
I'm consumed by my foible, you

words repeated like a mantra
develop a hollow luster, a poor habit
I commit to half-heartedly
knowing at my core
you're not coming back
not the You I know
fatigued, my grip unsteady
my mind is full of debris of us
blowing away in your prolonged distance
the wish to turn back time an impossibility

a not so happy valentine

"you're an amazing and chill person
I'm glad I met you"

when words cannot save us
hearts groan, sucked into
black hole oblivion
a bottomless limbo

this
is where we're left
with unmeasured fondness
when declaring love falls short
am I allowed to miss us?

losing serendipity

after you, I play all our minute memories like a
broken merry go round, unable to accept it was
chance, not circumstance, that bonded us.
dear you, I pen, but the unread texts stack
ever so high. my phone cracked, gone is my
Fairy Tail cover, the one you'd tease me was cliché, a
goodbye, like to you, I wasn't ready for. at
home we placed trivia bets, but of all our gambles
I never thought 'I miss you' would
justify dismissal of plans of camaraderie
music festivals, cross country road trips, drunk
hijinks
never did I foresee any of it without you.
only 17 weeks, but in my heart's pocket I store the
playfully coy grins we exchanged, no
quandary felt too overwhelming sharing in
raillery - the hockey player to my swimmer, the
storyteller to my listener, math genius to my creative
expression
tell me you didn't buy Civilization VI to best me, to
spend time with
universes I'd have explored with you, instead I
vacuum shards of snowflake shots, you
were my competitor, my car expert, my cheerleader,
so
exceptional to me, I still want
you next to me, engraved in a
zophorous for all time for memory's sake.

I loved you

I was with him when my ailment began
around you, I ached for more
without you, I ached for you

"a shiny new toy"
my mom, my friends, he
disparaged my sanity
"it's just a crush"
they couldn't fathom why I
clung to the flimsy idea of you

but my soul recognized you

my high school crush played
hockey on field and ice
he gave me my first skating lesson
and caught me when I tumbled.
we stayed up late at night
admitting our need to belong
and challenging each other
to trivia quests, the STEAM whiz was
outmatched by my entertainment knowledge

my first love was an
enthusiastic party goer
striking up conversations with strangers
an avid storyteller, I was always enraptured
he was keen on healthiness

but had a big secret sweet tooth
he always asked me to be his ride along
crushed me into him when I was sad
and left me chortling at his
goofy antics in his maroon Vans

my first boyfriend introduced me
to a world of digital gaming
emotional anime and pet cats
he admired my intellect
appreciated my caretaking ways -
and introduced me to you

it was like I knew you my whole life
the sparks with those boys
lit my way to you

they were wrong
they still are
I still do

roots

when I walked four miles round trip
from my house to my high school
crossing busy roads and passing traffic lights
my mother was livid at my impetuous action

on a trip back from the bathroom, I headed out to
a chocolate shop down the street from our stop
in Belgium; my dad left an unfinished meal
to demand how I could be reckless in a foreign
country

when I woke up early to go downtown to see
the Liberty Bell and Independence Hall
afoot and alone, he fretted and called me
several times to locate me for my safety

on my drive to you, I got lost in the bowels
of Newark Airport, in the deep trenches of
cargo units, far from the road to Jersey City
You checked in, with faith I was okay

"who have you become?"
"you've changed"
because of you I tapped into
who I'd always been
the curious adventurer
they couldn't accept

true love

my temper flares like I'm fourteen again
when I'm told every choice I make affects my future
my low self-esteem bites like I'm fifteen again
when my grades dip and trigonometry makes no
sense
my flippant attitude screams like I'm sixteen again
when becoming a swim instructor was not an
accomplishment

you should get help, my ex tells me
you need counseling, my mother commands

I am alone again like I'm seventeen
no one to talk to, text or tease
I am anxious again like I'm eighteen
new people to meet, but I don't know who to be
I give in to impulses again like I'm nineteen
all to fit in

you should grow up, my ex tells me
you need meds, my mother commands

I indite my woes like I'm fourteen again
now in my eighty-seventh journal
I lock myself away to cry like I'm fifteen again
now in my car instead of a bathroom stall
I go for long walks like I'm sixteen again
now around my apartment than school halls

I put myself out there like I'm seventeen again
now for new jobs instead of colleges
I try to start over again like I'm eighteen again
pursue a new path that befits my vision of creating
I fiercely hope for a brighter today like I'm nineteen
again

the layers of my past are my guiding guardian angels
a professional could advise
but the whispering wisdom remains
to accept all my bruised and beaten selves
is to love myself completely
in a way no one else can.

motherhood

Rani and Raja
Indigo, my beauty queen
Charming, my little king
fill me with unadulterated joy

I did love him
I loved you
but I was peppered with
the disillusionment love is a formidable
glue that can withstand any strife
he wanted more than I could give
you wanted nothing at all
I was not enough

dejected and brokenhearted
the cats' intelligent peridot and amber eyes
found me, claimed me
Indigo jumped into my arms
Charming insisted on head rubs
Indigo licked my forefinger
Charming took a nap on my foot
I waited a lifetime for a fated sign
in their resonant purrs I found it

Charming drinks tap water from sinks
Indigo peers judiciously from atop the refrigerator
Charming chases his tail like a teaser wand
Indigo yowls running up and down the stairs

tuckered out they find their way to me
plop on the bed, we cushion each other
their vibrant personalities and unconditional loyalty
have stolen my heart
they are my raison d'etre.

branded

I walked to the Revolver
the college tattoo parlor drew me in like
ghostly shadows under my sheets
when I stared at the inside of my wrists

much too long I was stained in
purple, black and blue splotches
up my arms like a Pollock painting
his tenderness resuscitated me

when my brain synapses fire rapidly
vultures waiting to kill any hope I have
and Jose Cuervo only makes me cry
I need another outlet and it can't be him

on a shredded stool, I waited cross-legged
foot tapping, but I knew I had to be
emblazoned with a symbolic reminder
to put myself first

my turn
the buzz of the electric needle, louder
than the searing cutting pinches
I dug my nails into my palm to steady myself

a heart entwined with my initial
open and hidden with a flip of the wrist
it wasn't enough to keep

from worrying about disappointing him

I added to my collection
rebel, with 3's instead of e's
for the power of three: me, myself and I
I need only meet my own expectations

like a phoenix, I arose
I said no, I expressed my dislike
I wore combat boots to stomp through
even if the ground wasn't solid

I never thought I'd return to that doorstep
five years later, least of all because of you
but your vanishing act left me
as vulnerable as before him

I asked for a semicolon with a cat head
when curveballs change courses, I must
go on for my children
the tears will heal.

self-soothe

open-ended mysteries turn me
into a restless insomniac
in a pursuit for closure
I stole flannels and jackets
as retribution for leaving
without a goodbye
I wrapped myself up
in proof my connections
were not illusory

I gave up my thievery
admonished as egocentric
why everyone leaves
nothing to hold on to
in my destined loneliness
I cling to my patterned pursuit

I bought a matching sweatshirt
a lifeguard hoodie to go with
his Ron Jon surf shop one
in my red fleece I float
reliving our beach day together
long walks and hand holding
watching dolphins and sunsets
imparting speculations of what could be
withstanding tides of salty water
before we crumbled like a dry sandcastle
now he is gone

but I have the sweatshirt
our love preserved for all time

I bought a robe fashioned
to resemble the haori worn
in Demon Slayer, the show you watch
an outerwear you'd wear to a rave
swatches of yellow and orange
with white triangles reminds me
of your pizza blanket,
your favorite food group.
oversized and lined with sherpa
it's warm, protective, like your bear hugs
now you are gone
but I sleep in the robe
my love preserved for all time.

letter to myself

Ayy, you. I hear you. stop
belittling yourself for
choosing him. over yourself. now you know -
don't settle. your
earnest worth is limitless.
for him to get stuck and shut you out
goes to show
he wasn't the one for you.
it's hard to believe, but being
jilted is NOT a pattern.
know that even if you're not popular, are a
loner in fact, does not
mean you are not loved.
names can be listed, but the
only one who needs to be
priority is you.
quitting him won't be easy, instead
reacquaint yourself with esteem. the
second chances you want to give him? give to
yourself.
trust in affirmations
understand what you want: a
valuable life of passion and creation, not
wasted on someone who doesn't stick around
X, cut him out. but you loved him, and you can't.
still,
You, I will love unwaveringly.
zap, in time, you will feel it too.

www.ingramcontent.com/pod-product-compliance
Lightning Source LLC
Chambersburg PA
CBHW051756130826
49812CB00033B/1171
* 9 7 8 9 3 5 7 2 1 1 0 5 5 *